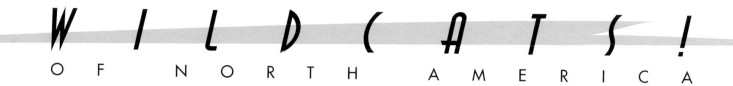

WILDCATS!

OF NORTH AMERICA

FERAL CAT

By Jalma Barrett
Photographs by Larry Allan

BLACKBIRCH PRESS, INC.

WOODBRIDGE, CONNECTICUT

Published by Blackbirch Press, Inc.
260 Amity Road
Woodbridge, CT 06525

e-mail: staff@blackbirch.com
Web site: www.blackbirch.com

Printed in the United States

10 9 8 7 6 5 4 3 2 1

Dedication
For the people of the
Feral Cat Coalition and for
all others who care and who
are helping to find solutions.

–JB and LA

Library of Congress Cataloging-in-Publication Data
Barrett, Jalma.
Feral cats / by Jalma Barrett ; photographs by Larry Allan.
    p.   cm. — (Wildcats of North America)
    Includes bibliographical references (p. 24) and index.
    Summary: Covers many aspects of these wild animals, including their physical features, reproduction and growth, habitat, social life, interactions with humans, and survival concerns.
    ISBN 1-56711-260-9 (lib. bdg. : alk. paper)
    1. Feral cats—Juvenile literature. 2. Feral cats—North America—Juvenile literature. [1. Feral cats. 2. Cats.] I. Allan, Larry, ill. II. Title. III. Series: barrett, Jalma. Wildcats of North America.
SF450.B37   1999
636.8—dc21
                                                                                98-3429
                                                                                CIP
                                                                                AC

Contents

Introduction—Not Your Average House Cat

They may look just like ordinary house cats, but feral cats are wild animals (*feral* means untamed or wild). They are the descendants of cats who once were domesticated. That means they were someone's pets. Feral cats can be ferocious and fierce. Often, they will bite and scratch someone who tries to touch them. Usually, they stay away from people. Feral cats do not trust humans. They live very much on their own.

There are nearly 40 million feral cats in the United States. There are also millions more in Canada and Mexico. Feral cats live all over North America, in the city and the country. In the cities they can be found in shopping centers, parks, and cemeteries. In the country, most farms have feral cats living in barns or other outdoor buildings. These cats aren't tame. You can't catch them or pet them.

Where Feral Cats Are Most Common

Feral cats may look like pet cats, but they are wild animals. This feral cat lost an eye, probably in a fight with another cat.

Where did all these wild cats come from? The answer to that question isn't simple. The major sources of feral cats are abandoned pets and litters of unwanted kittens. The more these abandoned animals *reproduce* (have kittens), the bigger the feral cat population gets.

The Feral Body

Feral cats are small, about the size of a pet house cat. Their tails are about 15 inches (38 centimeters) long, nearly the same length as their head and body. Feral cat colors are varied. They can be black, white, gray, orange, or striped—just like a house cat. Feral cats weigh between 6 and 13 pounds (2 to 6 kilograms). Cats have four rows of whiskers near their noses, and more on their cheeks and above their eyes. These whiskers help them walk safely at night through small spaces.

Charles Darwin, an English scientist, discovered that pet cats that had become feral increased in size and strength over generations. He also noted that those feral cats changed coloring. They became more gray with tabby (striped) markings—a return to the original colors of the house cat's ancestors.

Feral cats can be striped, gray, orange, black, or white.

Special Features

The tongue of a cat actually has little hooks on it. These hooks face backward, which helps the cat groom, or clean itself. The hooks pull dirt off the cat when it licks its fur. The hooks also act like little cups when the cat is drinking. They also help scrape meat off a bone when they're eating. Mother cats lick their babies a lot. This cleans the kittens and also shows them affection. In adult cats, licking is a sign of friendliness.

Cat tongues have hooks on them.
Opposite: The hooks help clean the fur when a cat licks itself.

Social Life

Feral cats live in *colonies*. That's a group of cats living together. A colony may contain animals both born wild and those recently abandoned. A colony of feral cats could have just a few members, or it might contain 35 or more cats. The size of the colony depends on the amount of food that is available to the cats. The colony size will get bigger if lots of food is available. It will also get smaller if little food is available. When a colony gets too large for its food sources, a small group of feral cats might move to another location, away from the original colony.

Most feral cats live near houses or other buildings. They raise their kittens in *burrows* (small tunnels), under buildings, or in other protected places. Many feral cats are fed by people who care about them—but they are still wild. The cats will come to get food. They do not develop any attachment to the people who feed them, the way house cats do with their owners.

Many feral cats in the country live in barns.

Feral cats will go near people only to get food.

Feral cats, like other wildcats, mark their territories with urine or with *feces* (droppings). The territory of a male is usually much larger than the territory of a female. A male might share parts of his territory with several females.

Life is difficult for feral cats. They generally live to be only 2 to 3 years old. Pet cats can live well into their teen years. The difference is that house cats receive good nutrition and good medical care. They also get protection from their owners, who care for them.

Feral Hunters

Feral cats spend most of their time hunting for food. If a feral cat colony gets too large, this hunting might actually destroy, or severely reduce, the native wildlife population of birds or other animals. Feral cats hunt by *stalking*, hunting and tracking in a quiet, secret way. Cats stalk by crouching close to the ground and waiting—sometimes for a very long time—for just the right moment to *pounce*, or jump.

Like other *predators* (animals who catch and eat other animals), a cat's eyes face forward. This allows them to see in a way that helps them locate prey. It also helps them judge the size of that prey and how far away it is. A cat's ears can move around. This helps it locate prey by the sounds the prey may make. A cat's sense of smell isn't too sharp. It plays only a small part in hunting.

Left and opposite: Feral cats hunt by stalking—quietly following and tracking prey.

The Food Supply

Voles, mice, shrews, and moles are important food sources for feral cats. One study showed that in 8 months 6 cats killed 4,200 mice in one 35 acre area! Cats also hunt birds, which make up about 20 percent of a feral cat's diet.

Feral cats have to catch what they eat or *scavenge*. Scavenging means to eat garbage or decaying matter. The cats are often found around dumpsters near fast food restaurants, especially at night.

Top: A feral cat eats its favorite prey, a mouse.
Bottom: Feral cats spend most of their time hunting for food.

How Long Does It Take to Become Feral?

The length of time it takes for a cat to become feral depends on the reason it has become wild. It also depends on the conditions of the cat's environment. Some cats begin living on their own because their former owners were cruel to them. These cats were already

partly wild, and will become totally wild very quickly. Other cats wind up living on their own because of an accident that forces them to take care of themselves. If they continue to live near people who do not threaten them, then they are feral cats that are *redeemable*. That means they can probably be tamed.

Cats living a feral existence have been known to become house pets again after a year or so, even though they might not have even seen a human face in all that time. Other feral cats are forced to take care of themselves in cold weather or live in poor shelter. They quickly become distrustful of humans. These types of feral cats reject attempts to be reclaimed by people. Kittens born to feral cats are born wild.

The Mating Game

Female feral cats will only let males come close when they are ready to mate. Feral cats have no specific mating season. Most feral and house cats can have two litters of kittens per year. In areas where winters are harsh, they usually mate in the spring and have only one litter. A male will bite the back of a female's neck while mating. The pair might mate several times over a period of days while the female is *in season*. This is when she's able to *conceive* (become pregnant with) a litter. In some litters, the smaller kittens might be the result of a later mating.

A female feral cat only lets a male come close to her when she is ready to mate.

Feral cat mating rituals involve chasing and, sometimes, rough behavior.

Kittens

Most kittens are born during the spring, between March and June. Sometimes this birthing period will last into August. Kittens, which weigh 3 to 5 ounces (85 to 142 grams), are born about 62 days after the parents mate. There might be 1 to 8 kittens in a litter. As with other wildcats, the mother raises the young without any help from the father.

Feral kittens are born about 62 days after their parents mate.

First Cat Lovers

Ancient Egyptians believed that cat eyes mirrored the sun and had the power to protect people.

The first people to bring wild cats into their homes as pets were the Egyptians. This happened about 4,000 years ago. Those first cats were probably captured as very young kittens and were raised and cared for by people. Cats were often shown in early Egyptian art wearing gold earrings and jewels. Egyptians even considered cats to be gods. The people of Egypt thought cats inspired feelings of fear, respect, and mystery. They thought a cat's eyes mirrored the sun and could protect people from the mysterious darkness of the night. Killing a cat became a crime punishable by death in ancient Egypt. The Egyptian word for cat is *miaw*.

Young kittens can take care of themselves at 1 month of age.

When the mother rubs her cheek along the sides of her kittens, she's marking them with her scent. Cats have scent glands on the sides of their forehead, on their lips, chin, and tail.

Kittens *knead*, or press their paws on, their mother's belly to make the milk flow when they drink. They will drink their mother's milk for 2 months. Related females will help *nurse* (feed milk to) the kittens of other females. They also watch and protect each other's kittens. At 4 to 10 days, the kittens' eyes open. Kittens are always born with blue eyes. It takes about 12 weeks before they get their real eye color. At 8 to 12 days, their ears open and they can hear. Kittens begin to stand and walk between 18 to 24 days. Young kittens can actually take care of themselves at about 1 month of age. When their teeth grow in place, they are able to chew their own food. At 12 weeks (3 months) their permanent teeth start to grow in.

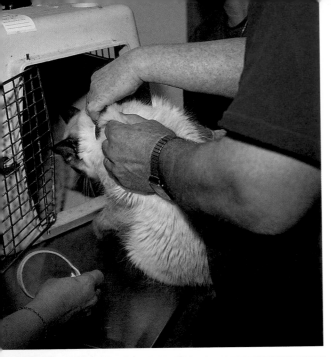

Feral Cats and Humans

Groups of people are banding together to help feral cats, and to control their rapidly growing population. One group is the Alley Cat Alliance in Baltimore, Maryland. Another is the Feral Cat Project in Rye, New York. The Feral Cat Coalition is in San Diego, California. These groups were formed to help feral cats. They provide the cats with food and have them *spayed* or *neutered* (removing the organs of reproduction) so they cannot have more kittens. Hundreds of cats can be spayed in just one day. The groups also give the cats shots to prevent diseases, such as rabies. The groups clean the cats' ears of mites and other matter, and comb their fur to remove fleas. Other medical problems are fixed as well.

Top: Volunteers in California provide medical treatment for feral cats.
Bottom: A cat receives a shave before being spayed.

These groups even try to get the wild cats to accept human contact. But it's very difficult to get feral cats to like people. It takes a lot of patience, but sometimes these groups can get kittens "social" enough to be adopted into homes.

Feline Facts

Name: Feral Cat

Scientific Name: *Felis catus*

Shoulder Height: 7" to 10" (17 to 25 cm)

Body Length: About 15" (38 cm)

Tail Length: About 15" (38 cm)

Weight: 6 to 13 pounds (2 to 6 kilograms)

Color: Varied

Reaches sexual maturity: Females at about 6 months; males between 5 to 10 months

Females mate: Twice a year

Gestation (pregnancy period): 62 days

Litter Size: 1 to 8 kittens

Social Life: Lives in colonies

Favorite Food: Mice and voles

Habitat: Varied, usually around buildings. Hunts in open fields throughout U.S., Canada, and Mexico

Glossary

burrows Small tunnels in the ground.
colonies A group that lives in the same area.
conceive To become pregnant.
feces Bodily waste; droppings.
feral Untamed or wild.
in season The time when a female animal is ready to reproduce.
neuter To remove the organs of reproduction in a male animal.

nurse To feed milk from a breast.
predators Animals who catch and eat other animals.
reproduce To mate and have kittens.
scavenge To search through garbage for food.
spay To remove the organs of reproduction in a female animal.
stalk To hunt and track in a quiet, secret way; usually following prey.

Further Reading

Arnold, Caroline A. *Cats: In from the Wild*. Minneapolis, MN: Carolrhoda Books, 1993.
Clutton-Brock, Juliet. *Cats* (Eyewitness Books). New York: Knopf Books, 1991.
Overbeck, Cynthia. *Cats*. Minneapolis, MN: Lerner Publications Company, 1984.
Ryden, Hope. *Your Cat's Wild Cousins*. New York: Lodestar Books, 1992.

Index